The Illustrated
DOG

The Illustrated DOG

Tom Howard

CHARTWELL
BOOKS, INC.

Published by
Chartwell Books, Inc.
A Division of Book Sales, Inc.
Raritan Center
114 Northfield Avenue
Edison, NJ 08818
USA

ISBN 0-7858-0178-2

Printed in Italy

FRONT COVER
A Terrier
by Marshall J. Fitz (1859-1932).

BACK COVER
**Whippet belonging to Frederick
the Great (1712-68)**
by an unidentified eighteenth century artist.

PAGE 2
Venus and Adonis
by Cornelisz van Haarlem (1562-1638).

PAGE 3
A Mastiff in an Alpine Landscape
by Conradyn Cunaeus (1828-95).

RIGHT
**A Water Spaniel and Two Jack Russells
by the Day's Bag**
English School (19th century).

Contents

Introduction

'Man's Best Friend' is such a well-established cliché that everyone knows for whom it stands and few would argue with its usage – except perhaps on gender terms to add 'and woman's'. The dog seems to have been a partner of humankind since the very earliest times and was almost certainly the first of the animals to become domesticated. Since then, it has played many varied roles, responding to the differing demands which have been made upon it. Its life has been dedicated to and dictated by us, its owners, and those critics who are concerned about dangerous dogs and hygiene problems should not blame the dog. Rather, they should blame humans – for it is they who are responsible for dogs. Happily, such problems shrink to insignificance beside the enormous benefits which dogs bring into our lives.

The artistic record reflects the changing status of the dog. It ranges from representations seen among hunting parties painted or scratched

BELOW
The Artist's Dog
by Charles van den Eycken, painted 1895.

ABOVE
**Two King Charles Spaniels Playing
with a Frog**
by Christopher Pierson (nineteenth
century). This breed was once called the
Bedford Spaniel but became known as the
King Charles after Britain's Charles II,
who made a great a fuss of them. Breeders
began to develop the breed as a smaller
dog with a much flatter face (the process
can already be seen in Landseer's painting
of two of these dogs). The old type
disappeared until, in 1925, an American
enthusiast offered prizes for those most
like the old type. To distinguish it from
the flat-faced King Charles, the revived
form is now a separate breed and known
as the Cavalier King Charles Spaniel.

LEFT
Puppies
a lithograph by Nobertine von
Bresslern-Roth (1891-?)

7

W. H. Trood 1891

on the walls of caves and rock-shelters by prehistoric peoples to the images which modern advertisers use to make us feel warm and friendly towards the products they are promoting. Dogs can be found in classical carvings, medieval manuscripts and the paintings of the Renaissance masters and at every period since. In kingly court and humble cottage, hunting in the desert or royal forest, in the farmyard and stable, with the flock upon the fell and even on the battlefield – dogs can be found in

scenes of every kind. They have been proudly painted alongside their masters and their mistresses and sometimes commemorated in portraits on their own.

Some painters are notable for their affinity with dogs and their special skill in portraying them. In the seventeenth and early eighteenth centuries dogs were an especial feature of the work of French court painters Alexandre-François Desportes and Jean-Baptiste Oudry, who often painted the hunting dogs of King

Louis XIV. In Britain, later in the eighteenth century, George Stubbs, famous for his paintings of horses also produced equally fine studies of dogs, and Thomas Gainsborough matches his magnificent portraits of people with those of the dogs they owned. Indeed, the first known painting which he signed and dated was a portrait of a Bull Terrier named Bumper! Sir Edwin Landseer, that great animal painter, was another master of dog portraiture, matched in his realism by his younger

contemporary the French artist Rosa Bonheur, while a succession of lesser artists, such as Cecil Aldin and Arthur Wardle, made a speciality of paintings dogs.

It is not only the animal painter who depicts the dog with accuracy and vitality. While other animals are sometimes poorly painted, the dog usually appears as a well-observed, familiar figure in genre painting and other works of art from every country, from the Bayeaux Tapestry to a Dutch interior, a Renaissance altarpiece to the

work of modern painters, such as David Hockney.

This selection of dogs in art shows many aspects of the dog and the text seeks to dip further into its association with ourselves, but dog-owners who make a close study of their own canine companion will know that there is always more to discover about its character and behaviour to enrich their on-going relationship.

Hot Pursuit
by William Henry Hamilton Trood (1860-99). This British painter was known for his paintings of dogs, most of which tended to have rather sentimental themes, but here he has contrived a lively picture with a range of different kinds of dogs. Among these nineteenth-century breeds appear to be Basset Hound, Bloodhound, Bulldog, Dachshunds, Cocker Spaniels, Springer Spaniel, Poodle, Fox Terrier, Jack Russell, Border, Cairn and a numerous other terriers — and greyhounds to set the pace.

The Partnership Begins

ifferent cultures around the world have a variety of stories to explain what brought humans and dogs together. Legends from Assam, Sri Lanka and other parts of the Indian sub-continent are similar. They all tell how the Creation God could not finish modelling man and woman in one day, so he made the dog to guard them overnight to prevent his work from being destroyed by evil forces. Another tale, of uncertain origin but generally attributed to North America, tells how God, after creating beasts and people, made a great chasm open between them. The beasts were all on one side and humans were on the other, but the dog ran to the edge and jumped across. His forefeet just reached the people's side and there he desperately hung. The first man heard him howling for help and, rushing to the chasm, held him and pulled him up. Since then the dog has been the comrade and friend of humans.

What really happened? We can never know, but we can guess. At first dogs were probably as much the quarry of the Palaeolithic hunter as any other animal, although too small and too fleet to be sought out. Dogs are still a food resource regularly found for sale in the food markets of southern China.

Both humans and canines hunted in groups or packs. Perhaps when one species saw another make a kill, they would follow to scavenge. Perhaps the smell of meat attracted dogs to the camps where hunters were butchering their kill. Their scavenging would remove the smelly remains of discarded parts, so their presence may have been tolerated and, in times of

ABOVE
A dog with a hunter, painted by prehistoric people on the wall of a cave.

plenty, they may even have been tossed a half-stripped bone to fight over.

Successful hunters observe everything around them very carefully. They would notice that the dogs had a good nose for game and be able to scent it long before the humans knew it was in the vicinity. They would realize that the dogs chased smaller scavengers away and grew restive and noisy if dangerous animals came near, acting as both a deterrent and an early-warning system. Then, perhaps, the dogs were deliberately given meat to make sure that they stayed around, incidentally providing a stand-by meal if prey was scarce and hunting failed.

Tolerance and then acceptance increased. Young puppies at the weaning stage were probably taken into the camp and fed, becoming semi-tamed and more manageable. They were also likely to be fleshier if they did have to be eaten. It has even been suggested that sometimes, in inversion

BELOW
The Dead Wolf
by Jean-Baptiste Oudry (1686-1755). Much of this French artist's work records the scenes and spoils of the royal hunts of Louis XV. Although here it is the quarry, the wolf is now generally agreed to be the species from which the domestic dog originated and the two can breed together. When domestication first took place cannot be precisely dated, but it must have been at least 14,000 years ago. How domestication took place is also a matter of conjecture. Our understanding of the dog is helped by remembering its wolf origins and the behaviour of the wolf pack.

of the Romulus and Remus legend, a woman who had lost her own new-born baby may sometimes have suckled orphan pups. (This idea is not so far fetched as it may seem. It may not be the habit in Los Angeles or London, but women who have lost a child at birth have been known to ease the build-up of milk by suckling a small animal.) Then, with dog and human children playing and growing up together, the dogs became imprinted as members of the human pack.

Did dogs join humans when they went out to hunt and rush to help finish off a dying beast that the weapon-wielding men had struck down? With their greater speed they could follow a wounded animal more

11

closely than people. They could track its scent, making it easier for the hunters to find. Did both species find that when they worked together they fed better than when they worked alone?

All this is conjecture – a likely possibility, but not established fact. Even the archaeological discovery of canine bones in close association with humans give us no clear proof of domestication. It is only when bones that show clear differences from wild canids are found in association with permanent settlements that it become easier to claim them as domestic dogs.

Magnificent prehistoric cave paintings make a feature of prey animals, such as bison, horses and mammoths, but, if they were made for hunting magic or for the purposes of religious ritual, dogs do not appear to have had a part in it. A Stone Age rock drawing in the Atlas mountains shows dogs accompanying a hunter who is aiming an arrow at some ostriches. There are paintings in Spain which have been identified as depicting dogs with hunters; some of the dogs appear to be held in restraint at the neck. A Scandinavian Bronze Age painting shows a pack of canids attacking a stag, and in the Tassili mountains of the Algerian Sahara shapes have been identified as representing two kinds of

dog – one looking like a greyhound and the other a heavier type. It has been claimed that they are pictures of dogs hunting and fighting. Fascinating though these images are, they still provide no clear evidence for dating or locating the domestication of the dog.

Whenever and wherever domestication occurred – and it probably happened many times in different places – people found a new role for the dog when hunters turned to herding. As they travelled nomadically from place to place, the dog was harnessed to drag a travois, a V-shaped form of sledge made of two poles with their ends trailing on the ground.

By the time the Egyptian civilization was established, not only did the dog already carry out hunting,

guarding, herding and haulage tasks, but a number of distinctively different types had been established.

Where had this domestic animal come from? The dog is a member of the genus Canis, along with wolves, jackals and the Coyote. They all belong to the same family of carnivores, the Canidae, which also includes the Fennec and northern foxes, South American foxes, Racoon-dog, Dhole, Bush Dog, Bat-eared Fox, Maned Wolf and Hunting Dog. Both the jackal and the wolf have been cited as the dog's ancestors, and it has been interbred with both species. Most scientists now agree that the most likely canine to have formed the first close association with mankind was an early form of the Asiatic Wolf, a subspecies which goes by the scientific name *Canis lupus pallipes*. There is evidence that a domestic form of dog was already in existence by 12,000 BC, so this association must have begun a good while earlier.

The dog, like the wolf, is a social animal. Wolf packs or groups of feral dogs have a hierarchy in which the weaker (and in the wild, the younger) members defer to the stronger and in which one dog takes precedence as pack leader. It is this which has made the human-dog relationship possible. The young dog looks to a leader and accepts the dominant human in that role. This is not necessarily the dominant member of the human pack. Father, mother or a grandparent in a larger family group may lead decision-making in a household, but the dog

A painting from the tomb of an official called Sennedjem in the Valley of the Kings, dating from the XIXth Dynasty (c. 1350-1115). It shows the god Anubis preparing the mummified body of Sennedjem for burial. Anubis accompanied the dead into the underworld and supervised the weighing of the heart in a balance against the feather of Ma'at – the symbol of truth. If the two sides balanced, the soul passed on to eternal happiness.

may give its prime allegiance to another person, even a child, if he or she establishes himself or herself in the position, reinforcing it by training. Establishing and maintaining dominance is important. A dog sensing a weaker will may respond as it would in its natural pack situation and make a bid to take precedence.

Dogs have the physical and sensory equipment of a hunting animal. They can run fairly fast, and with long endurance at a loping gait, and have a powerful forward leap that can carry them some way upwards, too. They have a highly developed sense of smell – probably a hundred times more sensitive than that of humans – which they rely upon much

more than sight. Although they will see movement at a distance, they will scent something or someone before their eyes notice it. Dogs are highly territorial, defending their own and their pack's patch. They have an aggressive response to any challenge or threat and strong loyalty to their pack.

Over the thousands of years since domestication, selective breeding has produced a great range of dogs in different shapes and sizes. They have been bred to exploit different characteristics that make them suitable for carrying out tasks useful to their owners. In no other species is there such a disparity between type and size as in the domestic dog; differences which range from the little Chihuahua to the Great Dane, the gentle Labrador to the fighting Pit Bull Terrier.

Egyptian carvings on green slate tablets dating from at least 4,000 BC show dogs of both mastiff and greyhound types. A different form of mastiff was developed in the Mesopotamian kingdoms. Known as the 'chained-up mouth-opening dog', it was obviously used as a watchdog. Later Egyptian art shows a dog like the modern Ibizan Hound, a curled-tailed spitz, a dog like a dingo, the mastiff from Mesopotamia, a Saluki type, a dog rather like a Basset Hound and dogs that suggest the Great Dane. There are also small terrier type dogs, but they are never shown in a working situation, which suggests that they were kept purely as companions. There are small spitz-type toy dogs, too, which must have been household pets.

ABOVE
A copy of a painted panel from a chest in the tomb of the Tutankhamun. This representation of the young pharaoh out hunting is probably very conventional, with ostrich, two kinds of gazelle, wild asses and hyena all being hunted by the ruler and his dogs. As in the other panels on this chest, which show his conquest of neighbouring nations, this is a symbol of his might and power over wild creatures.

By 3,000 BC small dogs, or 'sleeve dogs', were well regarded in China and the breeding skills that have since produced the Pekingese, Pug and Shih Tzu were already established. Quite different strains appeared in the Americas, long before Europeans introduced their breeds. There were Eskimo dogs, the Hair Indian dog of the Native Americans of the north and a small dog from the south which was bred for food – of which only the Eskimo type now survives.

As well as being a working animal and pet, the dog had a religious role in some cultures. In the ancient Greek and Roman world, it was often offered as a sacrificial animal. This was probably because it was inexpensive and available rather than for any ritual reason, although dogs were kept in the sanctuary of Asclepius, god of medicine, at Epidaurus, where their licking of the sick was supposed to heal.

Elsewhere, the ferocious Phoenician and Carthaginian Ba'al (the name means 'the Lord' and was applied to many local gods) was often represented with a dog's head. In parts of Africa carved dog fetishes were used magically to 'smell out' wrong-doers or to attack enemies. To the Gauls dogs were a symbol of lightning, and in Mexico, too, the dog was linked with the 'fire from heaven'. Among the most northerly Americans, the Aurora Borealis, the 'Northern Lights', was thought to be caused by sledge-dog teams carrying departed spirits to another life. There are many other links with death and the passage to another world: in Japan, Omisto was the dog-headed god of honourable suicide; in ancient Greece the three-headed Cerberus welcomed the dead and kept out the living at the entrance to the Underworld; in Mexico dogs were killed to accompany their masters to the other world; and the Egyptian god Anubis, another 'Conductor of Souls', was sometimes depicted as jackal-headed and at others as a wild black dog.

The main centre of the cult of Anubis was at Cynopolis, but he was worshipped throughout Egypt. He was usually depicted as a dark-skinned man with a dog's or jackal's head. He was originally described as the fourth son of Ra (the sun god), but was later said to be the son of Osiris, the Theban king who became god of the underworld, conceived when he was drunk and seduced by his sister Neb Het (or Nephthys). To add to the confusion, there was another jackal- or wolf-headed god called Wepwawet (or Up Uat) of Asyut in Middle Egypt, who was the guide of warriors and the avenger of Osiris. After the murder of Osiris, Anubis invented his funeral rites and wrapped his body as a mummy to preserve it. Thereafter he was thought to escort all dead souls to the underworld. Some representations of Anubis suggest a dog similar to the modern Ibizan Hound, others are more jackal-like, but he is always a canine god who accompanies humans in death, just as real dogs are at their side through life.

Hunting and Fighting Dogs

The walls of the palace of King Assurbanipal at Nineveh are carved with the exploits of this seventh-century BC Assyrian ruler overcoming his enemies and conquering new lands and in the royal hunting grounds. Scenes depicting offerings at the end of a lion hunt suggest that it may have had a symbolic significance, representing his strength and virtue overcoming the forces of evil and destruction represented by the lions. The carved reliefs include powerful mastiff dogs which were used in hunting and as part of the Assyrian war machine.

These mastiffs are of the type later known as the Molossian Hound, after Molossis, an area of northwest Greece famous for its dogs. It is the kind of dog the ancient Greeks used for hunting boar, bear and other large animals, but it was also employed for guarding and herding flocks. It has also been suggested that it is one of the ancestors of the St. Bernard, the rescue-dog of the Alps.

Phoenician traders have been credited with introducing such mastiffs to Britain from the Middle East. It was thought that an even more powerful British strain developed from them. However, historians and archaeologists now suggest that Phoenician ships never sailed so far, but that goods passed through intermediary merchants, so there is no evidence that the type was imported into Britain. What is fact is that the invading Romans found huge, ferocious dogs in Britain which so impressed them that many were taken back to Rome to fight in amphitheatres, where they made short work of the Greek dogs. The Romans called the British fighting dog *Canis pugnax* and a special Procurator, the

ABOVE
A bas-relief of the seventh century BC from Assurbanipal's palace at Nineveh. Mastiffs are led out by handlers, who also carry nets into which the dogs will drive the game. These and other bas-reliefs which decorated the halls of the Assyrian king, also show these huge dogs, of a type which became known as Molossian hounds, pulling down asses and taking part in lion hunts in the royal game park. The same type were also used as war dogs.

Cynegli, was appointed to find and procure such dogs to be sent to fight in the Roman arenas.

It is reported that the ruler of an Adriatic kingdom presented a fine Molossian hound to Alexander the Great. When it was matched against boars and bears, it refused to fight, so Alexander had it put down. The king, on hearing this, sent another like it with a message saying that the first

must have found his adversaries so weak he scorned to fight. He suggested these dogs be set against lions and elephants. This was done and, in single combat, the dog killed both lion and elephant. It won such approval from Alexander that when it died, he founded a city and gave it the dog's name, Peritas.

Reports of the largest mastiffs came from central Asia. Aristotle wrote of dogs 'crossed with tigers', such was their ferocity. More than 1,500 years later, the medieval traveller Marco Polo described dogs from Tibet as being as big as donkeys. Polo saw the Chinese Emperor out hunting with 10,000 dogs. Two of the emperor's brothers were appointed Chinuchi ('Keepers of the Mastiff Dogs'), each with the command of 10,000 men of whom 2,000 were dog handlers. At the beginning of the hunt they split into two bodies, 5,000 dogs to the left, 5,000 to the right. Polo wrote: 'They move along, all abreast of

one another, so that the whole line extends over a full day's journey, and no animal can escape them. Truly it is a glorious sight as the Lord rides a-hunting across the plains, you will see these big hounds come tearing up, one pack after a bear, another pack after a stag, or some other beast, and running the game down now on this side and now on that.'

A painted chest found in the tomb of the Egyptian pharaoh Tutankhamun has panels showing his soldiers and his mastiff war dogs overcoming Africans and Asians, and others which depict him out hunting with dogs. The mastiff continued to be used in war right up to the sixteenth century. Other breeds became more usual for coursing and hunting particular species to which their physiques were best adapted, although the mastiff continued to be used for hunting larger animals.

The dog has continued to play a role with the armed services. As well as being used as guard and watchdog, it was used as a message carrier during both twentieth-century World Wars. Dogs not only carried messages, but also ammunition, and the U.S. army used them to carry cylinders containing homing pigeons to take messages back to base. Dogs were used to detect minefields and to find buried civilians after bombing raids. They were used to seek out both survivors and enemy troops,

ABOVE
A Roman mosaic from a villa in Carthage in North Africa, dating from about AD 500, shows a hound hunting a boar.

LEFT
*A woodcut from **Anti-Bossicon** by William Lily and William Horman, 1521. Bear- and bull-baiting were popular spectator sports for centuries. Alongside the theatres where Shakespeare and his fellows presented plays in Elizabethan and Jacobean London was a similar building, where bears fought dogs or were harried in other ways. The place where it stood is still known as Bear Gardens. In Birmingham and other British towns, places called the 'Bull Ring' mark where bull-baiting took place, not the bullfights of Spain and Latin America.*

ABOVE
Hunting Wild Boar
by Peter Paul Rubens (1577-1640). The artist has shown a number of types of dog. Aggression and determination are needed to tackle quarry like this, but they are no proof against injury.

the early nineteenth century did not end such fights, but transferred attention to pitting dog against dog. Bulldogs were bred with terriers to create a faster more agile dog – the Bull Terriers. In 1835 dog fighting was also abolished in Britain (a year after it stopped in France). Although some dogs may still be illicitly bred as fighting strains, most of these breeds today have little trace of their warlike background. They are often well disposed not only to their owners and to children but to other dogs, although they retain their aggressiveness as guard dogs or if instructed to attack.

In Europe, lacking lions and with bears and wolves rapidly disappearing, the boar hunt – usually carried out on foot with a spear as the main weapon – was prized for the risks it presented, but it was the stag that was considered the noblest quarry.

There were those who trapped, snared and stalked animals for food, but, for the nobility, hunting was sport: the chase, following quarry and hounds on horseback, or waiting while hounds and beaters drove prey before them. In the sixth century hunting had become such a passion among the aristocracy that they even took their dogs into church with them. The scandalized Christian Fathers at the Council of Epone in 517 denounced such sacrilegious behaviour. The nobility responded by insisting that the church doors be left open so that they could hear the service from outside – with their dogs. From this came the custom of giving a blessing from the church door to the animals in general and especially to the dogs.

Part of the Church's original horror was because of tales that there were monstrous devil dogs, inspired perhaps by ownerless scavengers who dug up corpses, and of dog-headed men, the Cynocephali, who worshipped the witch queen Hecate. These Cynocephali were said to have been converted to Christianity by one of the Apostles – St. Andrew or St. Thomas – and there are icons of the Eastern Church which show a dog-headed St. Christopher.

especially in the Pacific where isolated Japanese soldiers were not always aware that the war was over.

The Japanese Tosa is a mastiff type, surprisingly agile for its size and weight, that is still bred as a fighting dog and matched in contest against its fellows. It is one of many breeds developed specifically for match fighting or baiting other animals. Even in countries where they are illegal, such contests are still held, albeit clandestinely. The legal constraints in

Britain on keeping the American Pit Bull Terrier are directly due to its import for dog-fighting and the risk that, even when kept as domestic pets, animals bred to be so pugnacious can be dangerous if not carefully disciplined and kept under control.

Bear-baiting and bull-baiting, in which captive animals were set upon by dogs for the sport of our callous forebears, produced breeds such as the English Bulldog and Bullmastiff. The banning of bull-baiting in Britain in

Rabies may have been a more valid source of fear; when a Church Council at Mahon in 585 forbade priests to keep dogs, even for guarding their houses, it was 'as much because of their noise and salacious behaviour as because of the poison transmitted by their bite'. A century before, Clovis, King of the Franks, had proclaimed that, although the owner of a rabid dog had no claim if someone killed it, 'if the owner denies the dog is rabid, it falls to the man who killed it to prove that the dog has been seen to attack animals and humans and that he has seen it bite its tongue'.

However, the attraction of hunting was not lost on later cardinals, bishops and other princes of the Church; even popes were known to take pleasure in the hunt. In the Middle Ages European rulers set aside great tracts of land as royal forests, hunting territory where strict laws protected their quarry from being hunted by common people. In England, for instance, King Canute introduced a law early in the eleventh century setting death as the penalty for anyone who hunted on Crown lands. If a stag was taken elsewhere, the miscreant was flogged and thrown in prison for two years; a second offence meant banishment. The Norman kings made penalties more severe. Instead of flogging, the punishment was to be blinded, and restrictions were brought in to ensure no dogs hunted on forest lands. Apart from shepherds' dogs, those kept in the vicinity had to be small enough to pass through a hoop 7 inches (17.5 cm) in diameter or be 'hambled' or hamstrung – have the great tendon at the hind knees cut. If

RIGHT
A Bear Hunt
by Carl Borromaus Andreas Ruthart, painted in the mid-seventeenth century. It shows several types of dog. One of mastiff type, which is attacking the central bear from the rear, has a spiked collar to give it protection. The dogs with more flattened muzzles on both the left and right sides of the picture have their ears cropped: this was to make them less susceptible to bites in the course a fight than the pendulous ears of most of the other dogs.

LEFT
Rat Catching at the Blue Anchor Tavern
by an anonymous nineteenth-century artist. Rat-catching was a timed event (the timekeeper with his watch is centre) with spectators betting on how many rats each dog would catch and kill. In the 1820s, a dog called Billy gained fame by killing 100 rats in only 5 minutes 30 seconds. The pits often had a metal baffle across the corners to prevent the rats climbing up, as one is trying to do here.

sheepdogs were found chasing game, a huge fine was imposed. Under Henry II, the mutilation was changed to a deep cut across the ball of the foot and then, less painfully, to the cutting off of three claws from one forefoot. Then, in King John's reign, the order went out that all dogs and mastiffs in the royal forests should be destroyed.

In France, Francis I issued a decree that all dogs belonging to farmers and peasants had to wear a heavy block of wood attached to their collars when outdoors to make it impossible for them to hunt – and if any were still caught hunting on royal land, they were hamstrung. Henry III of France banned the use of hounds and water spaniels by ordinary people and made any commoner caught hunting liable to the death penalty. This Henry had a passion for dogs – not hunting dogs but little Papillons, which he used to carry around with him in a basket hung from his neck!

Hunting developed its own rules and etiquette, and from the middle of the thirteenth century a number of treatises on hunting were written. The earliest are mainly concerned with conventional calls on the huntsman's horn and the cries with which the huntsman controlled the hounds; they reveal little about the dogs themselves. One written about 1350 by Alfonso XI, ruler of Castile and León, devotes space to kennelling. Another by Gaston Phebus, Comte de Foix, describes the hounds suited to particular quarry; its illustrations show the different types and show handlers checking their physical condition. In England in the early fifteenth century, Edward Duke of York, 'Master of Game' to Henry IV, wrote a book called *The Master of*

LEFT
The Dog Fight
by Thomas Rowlandson (1756-1827)
Two dogs are matched in the Westminster dog pit in London, while spectators restrain their own dogs waiting for a fight. The shouting and barking must have been deafening!

LEFT
Bulldog
by French naïve painter Camille Bombois (1883-1970) shows a French Bulldog, which has upright ears instead of the typical 'rose' ears of the Bulldog, and is only half the usual size. It has been claimed that this breed is an ancient Spanish fighting dog, but it seems more likely that this breed is a nineteenth-century miniaturization of the Bulldog. A massive jaw and receding nose made it easier for the Bulldog to hang on to the bull but still be able to breathe. Pushing its weight to the front of the animal made it more difficult for the bull to shake off. However, the short-legged modern breed in which these features are so well demonstrated was not fully achieved until after the prohibition of bull-baiting in Britain. In the past 100 years breeders have sought to eliminate the Bulldog's ferocity and have turned it into a good-natured, dependable breed.

Game, which gives more information about breeds and the care of dogs. However, the interest of all these noblemen is in the hunt – not in the dogs themselves.

Two similar miracles, linked with St. Eustace and St. Hubert, served as a warning to the hunting-mad not to let it take over their lives. Eustace was the patron saint of hunters. Formerly called Placidus, he was one of the Roman Emperor Trajan's generals. While he was out hunting his horse suddenly halted and a cross appeared between the antlers of the stag he was pursuing. A voice demanded, 'I am Christ, why do you persecute me? I have heard of your good works and alms-giving. Go seek the Christian bishop and be baptized.' So Placidus was converted and took the Greek form of his name, Eustachios. Eighth-century Hubert was hunting on Good Friday when a magnificent stag he had been following all day suddenly turned to face him. He, too, saw a cross between its antlers. He dismounted and he went down on his knees. The stag spoke, 'Why do you pursue me? Will you allow your passion for the chase to make you forget your salvation?' Hubert took up the religious life, became Bishop of Liège and, after canonization, also became a patron of the hunt.

The monks of the abbey dedicated to St. Hubert at Mouzon in the Ardennes developed a large, powerfully built breed of dog named after him. The St. Hubert Hound had a good nose and, although not fleet-footed like the greyhounds, was ideal for hunting deer in heavily wooded land. Each year the monks made a present of six dogs to the King of France, which ensured that all the nobles of the court learned of their qualities. The St. Hubert was the ancestor of the Talbot Hound, the type used by the Norman kings of England. The Bloodhound is probably its modern descendant.

Stag-hunting continued as the sport of kings for many centuries. Many varieties of hounds and other hunting dogs were bred, such as the Scottish Deerhound, bred for deer coursing in which pairs of dogs were

LEFT
Bitch with her Puppies
by Samuel de Wilde (1748-1832).
This is the type of dog which was
developed into the fighting breed that was
matched in dog fights in the nineteenth
century. The Dutch-born, British artist
became best known for paintings of actors
in their stage roles.

LEFT
Hound and Hunter
by American artist Winslow Homer
(1836-1910).
Hounds were expected to pursue their
quarry through whatever terrain they
encountered, including crossing a river.

slipped to bring down a stag or hind,
and the squat Dachshund, bred in
Germany to follow quarry such as
badgers, underground. Deforestation,
the Civil War in Britain and the
Revolution in France brought an end
to the great days of stag-hunting in
Europe but, at the beginning of the
eighteenth century, the kennels of
Louis XIV of France housed more than
1,000 dogs: a pack of Scottish hounds
for roe-deer, dogs from Champagne
for hares, Pyrenean Mountain dogs for
wolves and Anglo-French boar-
hunting dogs to set against large
game.

ABOVE
A life-size Chinese ceramic model of a hound from the Qialong period (1736-95).

RIGHT
*An illumination from **Le Livre de Chasse** ('The Book of the Hunt') by Gaston Phebus, Comte de Foix, which he began in 1387. The French chronicler Jean Froissart describes how Gaston and his wife Agnes would take 1,600 dogs of various breeds on their hunting expeditions. Here the huntsmen sound their horns to tell the rest of the hunt that the hounds are giving chase. The dogs here include a greyhound as well as a pack of St. Hubert type hounds.*

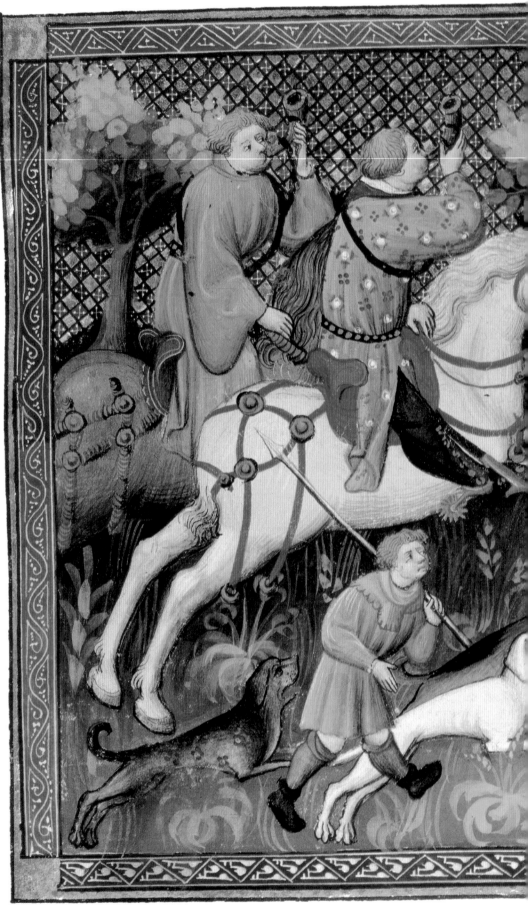

23

Guard and Herding Dogs

From the first, the dog's usefulness as sentry and guard would have been recognized. Every dog owner knows how very much earlier their animal is aware of the approach of friend or enemy and how joyfully or suspiciously it will signal that foreknowledge. Today, although household pets will all bark a warning and most would put up a good show in defence of their human pack and its property, most people want a friendly dog. Large, fierce dogs are usually kept for security purposes in industrial and similar premises, but they need very careful training and experienced handlers.

There are many tales of dogs defending territory, property and people, sometimes to the death. In ancient times, dogs are said to have saved the whole city of Corinth from a surprise attack. All but one of its 50 guard dogs were killed by the enemy, but the solitary survivor was able to rouse the city and give the alarm in time to repulse the attackers. In gratitude, the city erected a monument to the dogs who had died and made a silver collar for the survivor, inscribed with his name: 'To Soter, defender and saviour of Corinth'.

When the Roman city of Pompeii was excavated from beneath the volcanic ash that had covered it in AD 79, mosaics bearing the message *cave canem* (beware of the dog) were uncovered at the entrances of houses. They also included pictures of fierce dogs to warn off any intruders. In 2,000 years some things have not changed. Fears for personal safety and security are again making more private people think in terms of keeping more pugnacious breeds as house guards.

Sheepdogs and other herding dogs were at first mainly guard dogs, warning the herdsman of a marauding wolf or other predator. It is surprising that the dog could be made to identify its interest with a 'pack' of a different species, and even more amazing that it could be trained to round up and control sheep and cattle. All successful

ABOVE
A mosaic excavated at Pompeii. Not only mosaics of dogs were buried by the eruption of Vesuvius. Dogs themselves were asphyxiated by the poisonous gases and buried under the fall of ash. One, forgotten and left chained in the panic to escape, died still struggling to free itself. Another, which did not succumb to the fumes and starving to death, ate its dead master, whose bones bore its toothmarks.

ABOVE
Keeping Watch
by Alfred Duke (died c. 1905).
*The classic role for dogs in keeping with
Victorian sentiment: guarding a sleeping
child.*

RIGHT
*A coloured Chinese woodcut of 1873. The
Chinese Foo or Lion Dog, often seen in
ceramic form or as a big figure outside
temples and palaces, was a mythical
guardian combining the qualities of the
lion and the dragon. It has often been
suggested that the Pekingese was
deliberately bred in an attempt to emulate
their appearance. Despite their small
stature Pekes prove aggressive and
tenacious at any threat to territory, people
or possessions which they consider to be in
their charge.*

animal training has its roots in the
utilization of basic instincts, but one of
the great achievements of this kind
was the way in which our remote
ancestors managed to redirect the
dog's natural hunting instincts to drive
and isolate its quarry and employ
them to control the movement of
sheep and other herd animals without
following through to the attack.

The Roman Marcus Terentius
Varro, writing a treatise on farming in
the first century BC, paid considerable
attention to the training and treatment
of sheepdogs, which he considered
quite different in kind from those
suitable for hunting: 'To begin with,
you must obtain dogs of the right age:
puppies and old dogs are no good to
themselves or the sheep and they
sometimes become prey for the wild
beasts. They should be handsome in

25

form and of great size.... The bark should be deep, the jaw stretch wide and the colour preferably be white (they are then more easily recognized in the dark) and their appearance should be lion-like....

'Take care not to buy dogs from hunters or from butchers. Butchers' dogs are too idle to follow the flock, hunting dogs, if they see a hare or stag, will chase after it instead of after the sheep. The best dog is one bought from shepherds which has been trained to follow sheep or has no training at all. A dog develops a habit more quickly than other animals, the attachment to the shepherds which results from its familiarity with them

LEFT
The Mid Day Rest
by Walter Hunt (1861-1941).
But no rest for the dog! A collie watches
over the flock while the young shepherd
sleeps. A working dog's skill in handling
the sheep and understanding instructions
is much more important than its
appearance. The Border Collie, often black
and white and usually smaller than the
Rough Collie, had for centuries been a
nimble herding dog in the England-
Scotland border country. The breed is a
comparative newcomer in the show ring,
but it has been consistently winning
Sheepdog Trials since they began to be
held end of the nineteenth century.

BELOW
Patient Vigil
by Gourlay Steell (painted 1869).
The Rough Collie, a hard-working
sheepdog breed, was little known outside
the Scottish Highlands until Queen
Victoria made her first visit to Balmoral
in 1861. She fell in love with them and
took Rough Collies back to Windsor
Castle, so setting a fashion for them which
led to huge prices being paid for dogs on
both sides of the Atlantic. The Collie was
taken up by the show fancy and by 1895
seven different breed clubs had become
established, many of them sponsoring
collie-only shows. Breeders soon turned
the rough and ready working animal into
an elegant show dog.

is stronger than that which he feels for
the sheep.'

Varro considers diet, breeding and
rearing. To prevent injury by wild
beasts he recommends a collar: a band
of stout leather around the neck,

furnished with nails that have heads on them. Under these heads is sewn a piece of soft leather, so they do not hurt the neck. If a wolf or other animal has been wounded by such a collar, it makes other dogs safe from him, even those who do not wear one.'

He goes on to discuss numbers – one dog for each shepherd, more if the flocks graze or travel through areas with many predators. He suggests a pair, male and female, for flocks settled on a farm: 'For the same dog when he has a companion grows keener than before, and if one or other fall ill, the flock need not be without one.'

Many of the sheepdog breeds are white. These include the Italian Maremma, the Pyrenean Mountain Dog, the Hungarian Komondor and Kuvasz and the half white Old English Sheepdog. These are all large dogs and may share a common ancestor, probably introduced to Europe by early invaders from Asia. They have been more important as guardians of the herd than for skill in rounding up the sheep. Their white

coats made them easy to distinguish from a wolf, which would have been the main predator on the flock, and perhaps helped sheep to accept their presence more calmly.

The lupine appearance of the German Shepherd Dog emphasizes the way in which the predator has been turned into the protector although, in fact, dogs such as the Elkhound are probably more close relations of the Wolf. The Groenendael, Tervuren and Malinois, all from Belgium and somewhat similar in appearance to the German Shepherd, are all fine herding dogs. Collies, however, although now often kept as show dogs and pets, have probably excelled all other breeds in herding skills. There are some 70 breeds of sheepdogs and herding dogs around the world today, although many of them no longer work for a living. Of them all, the Border Collie is probably the most versatile and widely used. It was recognized only comparatively recently as an official breed; as it was bred for working with sheep rather than for looks, it did not fit a Kennel Club specification.

LEFT
A Sheepdog, Fields Beyond
by Reuben Haliom (nineteenth century). An Old English Sheepdog, a breed that, like the Bearded Collie and many of the European continental sheepdogs, was used as much for driving sheep to market as for handling them on the farm. The modern show breed has tended to become much bigger and more luxuriant in coat.

Painters rarely took shepherds and their dogs as a subject. Classical mythology offered the subject of the Judgement of Paris, with the Trojan prince in his shepherd guise as he presented the golden apple to the goddess Aphrodite. A shepherd and his flock sometimes formed a minor detail in a classical landscape by Claude, but sheepdogs appeared only occasionally along with their shepherds in scenes of Christ's Nativity. In the seventeenth century they appear in some of the genre pictures of the Le Nain brothers, but the wealthy, who were the artists' patrons, were much more interested in the hunt than in the flock. In the nineteenth century, sheepdogs appear in naïve pictures by country limners and, increasingly, in the work of painters celebrating rural life or the loyalty symbolized by faithful dogs. In the popular imagination they are now a favourite image for evoking such ideas.

LEFT
The End of the Day
by Wright Barker (1864-1941).
The luxurious coat of one of these dogs, painted towards the end of the nineteenth century, already looks more like the modern form of the Collie, which a century and more of selective breeding has refined and emphasized. Both a short-haired form and a long-haired miniature are now recognized as separate breeds: the Smooth Collie and the Shetland Sheepdog (or Sheltie).

RIGHT
The Royal Wedding
by Ditz (contemporary artist).
The Corgi became a favourite breed of King George VI, Queen Elizabeth the Queen Mother and Queen Elizabeth II, which greatly increased its popularity as a family pet – although it is not the best tempered of dogs. This tongue-in-cheek contemporary watercolour reflects its royal associations, but both these Pembroke Corgis and the slightly rougher-coated Cardigan Corgis were originally hard-working dogs used for driving cattle.

RIGHT

The ladies in this eighteenth-century French painting have been travelling in a carriage drawn by dogs. For a time, it was fashionable to put dogs in harness to draw carts for children, and they were regularly used for deliveries of milk or even on a mail round. Traffic growth in towns, especially in London, led to their prohibition in Britain in the mid-nineteenth century, but their use continued until the mid-twentieth century on the continent. It survives in a carting competition for Bernese Mountain Dogs at Crufts Dog Show.

Sledge dogs have been used by the Inuit for centuries but, sadly, the last husky teams have now left Antarctica and even the huskies on which the Inuits of the north depended for centuries have now been largely replaced by mechanized transport, although sledge-dog racing survives as a sport.

ABOVE

A detail from an engraving after a drawing by Thomas Rowlandson (1756-1827). Dogs were used on treadmills to turn small machinery and domestic appliances such as this cooking spit, set to rotate food before a kitchen fire.

Though breeding may, perhaps, pass on the intelligence and strong to control the flock that makes a good sheepdog, each dog must be individually trained to ensure that this is used for herding not for hunting. A youngster may be able to learn from other dogs, but can easily acquire bad habits. While obedience training for most dogs is to make them obey commands unquestioningly, a sheepdog must learn to think for itself and use initiative. The guarding breeds must make their own decisions about handling predators, keep sheep from straying, make sure they are kept separate from adjoining flocks and draw their shepherds' attention to any sheep that are sick or in difficulty. A main task for German Shepherds and Belgian sheepdogs, used in areas where crops were seldom fenced, was to keep sheep from going among them; this demanded day-long, tireless loping around the flock rather than bursts of speed.

As well as all the usual obedience commands, sheepdogs usually learn to respond to called, whistled or physically signalled commands and to respond to instructions at long distance. Its belly-to-ground crawl forward, its sudden rush after a sheep that has separated from the flock and the fixed hypnotic glare – known as the 'eye' – with which the dog controls the sheep are elements of its hunting technique turned to new purposes.

Dogs would control the herd on migration or when moving from pasture to pasture; these days they often have to thin them out to a long line to allow vehicles to pass on roads. They would also have helped to drive the sheep to market. Droving dogs took both sheep and cattle on long journeys from their home farms to big cities. The best type for driving cattle were lively smaller dogs, which could nip the cattle at their heels but slip nimbly between them without getting kicked. Some breeds, such as the Australian Heeler or the Corgi, which used to drive Welsh cattle some 300 km (180 miles) to London's Smithfield market, were developed specially for the task.

Sight Hounds

Sight hounds, or 'gaze' hounds and wind hounds as they are also called, are quite distinctive in their shape from other hunting dogs. With their narrow, streamlined heads, slim bodies with elongated arched backs, tucked-up loins and deep chests, they are built for speed. Long-legged and muscular with well-developed hearts and lungs, they can run at speeds of nearly 65 kph (40 mph) – the fleetest of the dogs. Breeds range from the Irish Wolfhound to the Borzoi or Russian Wolfhound, the Afghan, Saluki and the Greyhound, with smaller versions in the Whippet and the daintily diminutive Italian Greyhound.

Dogs of greyhound and saluki type are frequent in the art of ancient Egypt and were used by the Egyptians for hunting gazelle. They were favourites with Arabs and Persians who bred them with care and great attention to pedigrees, which have been kept pure for thousands of years. Most dogs were considered unclean by the Semitic peoples, but the Saluki was an exception; the nomadic Bedouin even allowed Salukis to enter and share their master's tent.

In the relatively unforested terrain of north Africa and the Middle East there was no need for these dogs to hunt by scent, for they can see their prey. Many will lose interest in the chase the moment that its object goes out of sight. They were ideal for falconry, able to see the hawk strike in the air and then locate where the prey had fallen. Trained falcons were also used by Arab sheiks to harass gazelle which their dogs had singled out from the herd.

Interest in coursing, whether for gazelle and antelope or for smaller,

ABOVE
An ostrich-feather fan from the tomb of the Pharaoh Tutankhamun, dating from about 1,340 BC. The feathers were inserted to radiate from this metal holder. The pharaoh is shown hunting ostriches with bow and arrow. Were the dogs used just to flush out the birds for the archer or were they also used to course them? The flightless ostrich can run at speeds of up to 60 kph (37 mph) and can strike a powerful blow with its claws, making a more formidable quarry than would at first appear.

fast quarry, such as hare, is less in the killing of the prey than in comparing the ability of the dogs involved. When the quarry is spotted or shortly after the release of captive hares, the hounds, usually a single pair, are 'slipped' from their restraints and their speed and performance matched.

The Roman Flavius Arrianus, writing at the beginning of the second century AD, advised that puppies should not be taken coursing until they are two years old to avoid potential harm through undue physical strain before they are fully grown. He recommends that no more than two dogs be released and that the hare be given a good start because, when first put up from its form, it is terrified and confused by the noise from the spectators and caught too readily, giving no sport. He continues:

'suffered to run some distance and collect her spirits, she will lift up her ears and stretch out with long strides from her seat, the dogs directing their course after her with great activity of limb, as if they were leaping, affording a spectacle worthy of the trouble that must necessarily be employed in properly breeding and training these dogs.'

A running dog's speed comes from its back and hind legs, and a longer back often makes for a better stayer than sprinter. Speed depends upon the length and rapidity of the stride. A greyhound's running gait is like that of a cheetah: a series of long leaps in

which it pushes off with the hind legs and becomes fully extended in the air with the forelegs stretched in front. After the forelegs touch the ground, the hindlegs are drawn forward under the body to land in front of them, ready to spring off again. This demands great power in the muscles not only of the rear legs, but also those of the back, which must expand and contract like a spring.

The Whippet, once known as the 'snap dog' because it competed in matches to see which dog could snap up the greatest number of rabbits, became a racing dog without a living prey to chase. Instead, it was trained

Coursing at Maymill

by B. Blake (early nineteenth century).
The object of coursing is competition
between dogs rather than the killing of
prey. The handlers, who are on foot,
release dogs in pairs. Lower down the hill
another couple are waiting their turn to
compete. There are two ways of coursing.
Open coursing allows the pursuit of any
hare that can be discovered over
undetermined territory; close coursing
(illegal in Britain for 150 years) takes
place within fixed boundaries or in a
fenced area and dogs are slipped after
captive hares have been released.

Greyhounds Giving Chase

by Arthur Wardle (1864-1949),
an artist especially known for his dog
paintings. Here the dogs have put up a
rabbit. Coursing is not simply based on
which dog first reaches and kills the hare.
Points can be scored for speed, for the 'go-
by' (when a dog a clear length behind
another overtakes it on a straight run and
gets a clear length ahead), the turn (when
the hare turns not less than a right-angle),
the wrench (when the hare turns less than
a right-angle), the kill and the trip (an
unsuccessful effort to kill).

to race towards a piece of cloth that was shaken 180 metres (200 yards) away at the end of individual lanes marked out with string.

Racing greyhounds with a moving, inanimate lure seems to have been tried out first in 1876 at the Welsh Harp on the outskirts of London. An artificial hare was pulled along a grooved runway on a wire hand-wound on a windlass. The course was straight and, to anyone who knew the dogs' form, the result too predictable to make it a good sport to bet upon, so it did not catch on. To overcome this problem, the promoters developed a circular track, taking out a patent for it, but lack of interest and opposition from the coursing fraternity made them drop the whole idea.

Three Greyhounds
painted by Benjamin Cam Norton in 1862. The dogs have not been identified, but, since this artist painted mainly to commission, they are likely to be portraits of specific animals, probably winners of major prizes for the owner who commissioned the painting, which shows them against a background of typical coursing country.

Some decades later the idea was taken up in the United States by Owen Smith, an Oklahoma farmer who had been summoned for coursing hare in an enclosed paddock. He discovered and acquired the patent and organized races. Tracks at Tucson, Arizona, Emeryville, California and Oklahoma City have all been claimed as the first modern style track. Charles Munn, an American sportsman, took the sport back to England and 'The Dogs' has had a wide following ever since.

The modern greyhound stadium enables thousands of people to watch a sport that was formerly restricted to comparatively small numbers, and the races do not end in the cruelty of an animal being torn to pieces. However, a great many dogs are bred that prove to have no chance of being winners and in which their owners have no subsequent interest, so that they often are put down. Similarly, dogs are rarely raced beyond their fourth or fifth year and they have no future after their racing days are over. Various organizations have been set up to find homes for retired greyhounds and, since any with a tendency to fight are usually eliminated before trying them in a racing career, they usually make gentle, affectionate pets which are good with other dogs. However, it may not be wise to trust them with cats or other animals of the size they have been trained to chase.

The elegance of the greyhound family's physique makes them an attractive subject for the painter and sculptor. They often appear with other dogs in hunting scenes from the early and late Renaissance. The little Italian Greyhound also makes a frequent appearance. There is a pair at the centre of Antonio Moro's 1552 portrait of Mary I of England and her husband Philip of Spain and, a decade later, in the middle of Paolo Veronese's painting *The Wedding at Cana*. No fewer than five are gathered around the skirts of Anne of Denmark, wife of England's James I, in her portrait by Paul van Somer. The breed was also a popular subject for ceramic figures with fine examples from many European potteries. Coursing is a frequent subject for English nineteenth-century sporting prints and paintings. The aristocratic owners of fine dogs commissioned portraits, which range from one of the few surviving works by Benvenuto Cellini, a small relief of a Saluki, a breed which also appears in several paintings by Veronese, to a double greyhound portrait by Gustave Courbet, as well as by those artists who have specialized in dogs.

BELOW
Exercising Greyhounds
by George Goodwin Kilburne (1839-1924). Coursing greyhounds and modern racing dogs need plenty of regular exercise. If a young dog is intended for the track, its exercise programme must be carefully planned to match it to the development of its racing muscles. To put them under too much strain could cause injuries which would ruin its chances of success on the racetrack.

Scent Hounds

Hunters in well-wooded lands require hounds which can track, find and flush out game, either to chase and bring down themselves or to provide a target for the hunter. These dogs bring their quarry to bay by their persistence rather than their speed. Each region tended to develop its own types of hound suited to the terrain and the available game, but both medieval and Renaissance pictures suggest that the same hunt might use several kinds of hounds. These could include dogs that were mastiff-like, the St. Hubert type, greyhounds and even spaniels. Although generally there were smaller hounds for hunting hare and smaller game and large hounds for hunting the bigger animals, whatever quarry the hounds put up, that was what they hunted. By the end of the seventeenth century this had begun to change with its becoming more frequent for a pack of selected hounds to be kept for hunting a specific type of prey.

Hounds that follow their prey by scent rather than sight are not usually so swift as the greyhound type – but they do not need to be. They follow their noses and can take a more leisurely pace, relying on their persistence to wear out prey which cannot keep going for so long.

The pattern of hunting changed in Britain in the seventeenth century following the Civil War, and in France after the Revolution. During the Commonwealth period Oliver Cromwell broke up Britain's great deer parks and, in the years that followed, hunting began to turn to other quarry. By the end of the century, fox-hunting was well

established among country gentlemen, although among local squires and farmers hunting hare was the principal sport well into the eighteenth century. With the fall of the monarchy in France, the hunting privileges of the aristocracy were abolished and commoners and peasants were able to hunt as freely. Meanwhile the kennels of the aristocracy, with their thousands of hounds, largely disappeared.

As the countryside became more densely settled and enclosed, the larger animals of the chase disappeared or were restricted to wilder regions. Without the protection of the royal parks and forests, the numbers of deer became far fewer. The emphasis moved to smaller types of dogs for hunting smaller prey. The smallest is the Beagle, now about 40 cm (16 inches) high at the withers, but these dogs were once so small that they could be carried in the pocket of a huntsman's coat. Originally, the Beagle was probably used mainly for hunting fox and similar prey, but increasingly it became a dog for hunting hare, the followers usually on foot, or for finding hares for greyhounds to course. In the United States and Canada it has more recently been used after the cottontail rabbit. Beagles may run in packs, but often just one or a couple of dogs are used alone.

The Harrier is larger but otherwise very similar to the Beagle. As its name suggests it, too, was used for the hare. It was developed specifically for this and is also usually followed on foot. In recent times it has become a popular dog for drag hunting, and then the huntsmen and huntswomen usually ride. Drag hunting does not involve a live quarry. It consists of laying a trail for the hounds to follow by dragging a scented bag along the ground. It gives

LEFT
Arthur Edwin Way
by George W. Horlor (fl. 1849-91).
A portrait of a country gentleman, dated 1852, smartly turned out in hunting 'pink' and with his fine hunting horse and favourite hounds.

41

all the pleasure of watching a dog at work and the exercise of riding or walking in the countryside without the cruelty of an animal's being killed with which blood sports culminate.

Larger still, the Foxhound is the third in this group of very similar dogs. Although a lighter-boned and speedier hunting dog than the St. Hubert type hound had been known much earlier, the Foxhound was developed mainly in England from the time when more people turned to hunting foxes. The first Foxhounds imported into America are said to have arrived in Virginia in 1650 and were set to hunt the grey fox, racoon and other prey. However, some sources prefer to date their establishment there from a pack Lord Fairfax took across the Atlantic in 1738, a few years after the introduction of the red fox from Europe.

In art, the fox-hunting scene became a popular genre, especially in Britain, for many country gentlemen became fanatic members of the hunt. The 'pink' coats traditional with many hunts and the ritual of the meet offered subjects that conjured up a romantic and colourful image of country pursuits and 'olde England'. As a winter subject, it was ideal for popular prints and Christmas and other greeting cards which began to appear from the middle of the nineteenth century.

America developed its own distinctive breed of American Foxhound, and dogs of similar type appeared in other countries. George Washington was an enthusiastic

BELOW
Otterhounds
by Sir Edwin Landseer (1802-73). Otterhounds can follow a scent on land that is ten or 12 hours old and in water track the otter by its 'wash', the faint trail of bubbles which it leaves as it swims underwater. Powerful swimmers, able to keep up pursuit in water for as long as five hours, their thick woolly undercoats and coarse outer coats enable them to cope with the freezing cold water.

42

The Otterhounds
*by John Frederick Tayler (1802-89).
The otter became so rare in Britain that
hunting it was banned as a conservation
measure. This put the continuation of the
Otterhound itself in doubt. It is a breed
that needs plenty of exercise and its size
and development as a dog dedicated to
following a faint scent to the exclusion of
all else does not make it an ideal pet.*

hound breeder and used hounds from
France to improve his stock. Some of
the original 1650 strain were the
foundation line for the American
Coonhound.

Linked more clearly with the St.
Hubert Hound and its near relation
the Bloodhound, are the short-legged
Basset Hounds. These dogs, whose
scenting powers are probably equal to
those of the Bloodhound, are low-
slung, but strong and bulky and ideal
for working in dense cover. They were
developed in France, where many
variations exist as separate breeds, and
were not known in Britain or America
until the late nineteenth century.

Although these breeds are
probably the most generally known
worldwide, there are many other local
hunting breeds, from the Swedish
Hamiltonstovare, usually used for
tracking on its own rather than in a
pack, to the Brazilian Rastreador, used
for hunting jaguar.

The Bloodhound, which many
identify directly with the St. Hubert
Hound (its name reflecting its pure
blood rather than any taste for gore),
has survived while most of the other
medieval and Renaissance types are
known only through descendant
breeds. It can be a very gentle dog and
although its superb tracking qualities

have been used for centuries to track down criminals and missing people, it is far more likely to lick them with joy when it finds them than to attack. Bloodhounds have been recorded as successfully following a scent more than a week old and none can better them. However, for a police dog that is required to track and then attack and restrain a dangerous criminal, breeds such as the German Shepherd are more frequently used.

The skills that made the dog so useful to the hunter in leading him to the kill and in tracking are now channelled to save lives by rescuing people buried under an avalanche or a collapsed building and for fighting some of the evils of modern society.

The St. Bernard, a rescue dog as famous as the Bloodhound for finding people, probably traces its ancestry back to the Molossian type, and was used as a watch dog rather than a hunter. It is not only the scent hounds whose highly developed sense of smell has proved of use to man. In recent years, Labradors and other retrieving dogs have shown an aptitude for sniffing out drugs and explosives and are now extensively used to combat both terrorism and the drug trade.

RIGHT
An Edwardian hunting scene
painted by Edward Algernon Stuart Douglas (1840-1892)
in 1906, presents the combination of horses, foxhounds and the soft misty landscape enlivened by the bright colours of the huntsmen's coats which made such pictures so popular as an evocation of traditional country life. The huntsman on the dappled grey has stopped to open the gate and the hounds have not gone bounding through, so it seems unlikely they are on the scent. Foxhounds must be very strong and hardy. If not taken to the meet by motor transport, they may have to cover 20 km (12 miles) before the hunt even starts and then, in a full day's hunting, have to run for up to another 80 km (50 miles).

Through the Fence
by Arthur Charles Dodd (exhibiting c. 1878-90).
This hunt has clearly found a fox and the pack is eagerly following the fresh trail. Gazehounds run silently, but these dogs bay with excitement when hunting a line. Experienced hunters will recognize the sound of individual hounds as they 'give tongue', identifying which dog has first picked up the scent and when another dog has challenged or taken the lead.

BELOW
Hunted Slaves
by Richard Ansdell (1815-85).
A breed known as the Cuban Hound was thought an especially good tracker and kept in the southern States of the U.S. for hunting down black slaves who ran away from their plantations in the years before the Proclamation of Emancipation. In Europe in the Middle Ages a manor or village might make use of a Bloodhound for finding a runaway serf or tracking down a criminal.

Sporting Dogs and Terriers

In past centuries, the dogs who drove prey forwards to waiting archers or the first firearms or to set up birds for the falconer were probably the same hounds as those used in the chase. Some, however, would have been picked out for their special characteristics and, eventually, breeds emerged which offered very particular skills to aid the hunter. In the Middle Ages these were the spaniels: springer spaniels, which would 'spring' the birds or game either for the hawk or to drive them into nets, and 'setter' spaniels which would search for birds and crouch or sit when they scented them close by. Charles IX of France set great store by his *chiens blancs du roi* ('white dogs of the king') which were water retrievers. One pair, Courte and Caron, were especially regarded. Courte used to eat from the king's own plate. Her hide was made into royal gloves when she died so that she would still be with him. When Caron died the whole Court was ordered into mourning for a day.

Later came the pointers, dogs which froze stock-still, using their noses to point the direction of hidden game. Pointers are often said to have come from Spain, and there is a tradition that the French pointer (Braque Française) arrived in England as a present to King James I from the King of France. The modern Pointer breed, however, was an English creation. France has several of its own pointer breeds, such as the Braque d'Auvergne and the pointing griffons. German breeds include the Poodle Pointer, the Italians have the Spinone and the Hungarians the Vizsla (which looks little changed from dogs shown

in a fourteenth-century manuscript on the art of falconry). There are many more, a number of which combine pointing with other gundog skills.

Both pointers and setters were expected to perform another task: to find the fallen bird and either guard it or retrieve it. To supplement their skills, many other breeds and cross breeds were employed in this task. As a result, a specialist was produced – the most recent group of the birddogs or gundogs: the retrievers.

The use of firearms instead of arrows or hawks made all these types of dog even more important. At first, the reloading process was very slow, so if the game was flushed before the hunter was ready, that shot was lost. The pointer and setter could ensure that the hunter was prepared in time.

ABOVE
Waiting for the Guns
by Basil Bradley (1842-1904).
A gillie with Gordon and English Retrievers waits on the hillside for the sportsmen to arrive to begin the day's shoot. These dogs will have been trained to work to the guns, whoever makes up the shooting party.

RIGHT
A Gamekeeper with Dogs
by Richard Andsell (1815-85).
The dogs are a pair of working setters and a black and white pointer.

The development of increasingly reliable and accurate guns led, by the end of the seventeenth century, to 'fowling pieces' being produced; these made it possible to shoot birds in flight. Hawking was frequently done on horseback, whereas the gun was usually fired on foot and sometimes from a fixed position or a punt. Although dogs had previously helped to find where a hawk had dropped with its kill or where the bird had fallen and, perhaps, retrieve it, the horseman had been able to ride over with reasonable ease. For hunters on foot it was more important to have a good retriever; if the quarry fell in water the dog must swim out and bring it back.

The Newfoundland is a water dog of much larger size and very different type from the retrievers and spaniels. An excellent swimmer, it was used for haulage and pulling nets from the sea, as well as helping fishermen in the water. The Labrador, from the same rocky eastern coasts of Canada, is another waterdog that was taken up as a gundog in Britain.

Further south on the Atlantic Coast, the Chesapeake Bay Retriever developed as the United States' own

ABOVE
Gundogs Flushing a Duck
by Abraham Hondius (1625-95).
One of these two is of vaguely setter type but, although the seventeenth century saw the beginning of the development of more specialized gun-dogs, these cannot be placed in any known breed and are an indication of the general-purpose dogs which many would have used. Indeed, these dogs could be working with falconers not with guns.

RIGHT
Partridge Shooting at Six Mile Bottom *by John Frederick Herring, Senior (1795-1865).*
A good birddog marks where a bird has fallen, but does not set off to retrieve until it has been given the command. At first it was probably sufficient for a dog to find and bring back dead and wounded game, but now, as well as having strong jaws to carry the bird, a dog must have a 'soft' mouth. It must grip the bird gently so that the carcass is not damaged by its teeth.

retrieving breed. It is a fine birddog, ideal for waterfowling.

Sportsman and dog had to understand each other perfectly and it is not surprising that owners came to

hold their dogs in high regard. Nor is it surprising that they often had a favourite gundog included in a portrait or even commissioned a separate portrait of their dogs. Among the most famous must be the triple portrait of three Braques Françaises, the favourite spaniels of Louis XIV of France, painted by Françoise Desportes, while English painters, such as James Ward and George Stubbs, painted many studies of sporting dogs, some showing dogs in the act of flushing game or holding the pointer's pose. French painter

Sir John Nelthorpe Shooting with Two Pointers
*by George Stubbs (1724-1806).
This English artist, who studied anatomy and dissected animals to understand their structure better, is acknowledged as one of the world's greatest animal painters. His dog portraits – and they are individual animals, not general types – range from water spaniels and spitz to foxhounds and poodles. His pointers are a little heavier than the modern dog, but the breed type is clearly recognizable. The moment a good pointing dog has established the location of game, it will freeze, lined on the quarry to indicate where it is, often halting with a paw in mid air.*

ABOVE
Terriers Rabbiting
by Arthur Wardle (1864-1949)
A pair of Wire-haired Fox Terriers by a twentieth-century painter celebrated for his meticulously observed dog portraits. Wire-haired and Smooth-haired Fox Terriers are now considered separate breeds. Both were bred as tough working dogs. They had to move fast to keep up with the hunt, ready to go into action, should the fox go to ground, following it down into its earth to bolt it out to the waiting pack of hounds.

Constant Tryon is another who caught the pointer's character, and nineteenth- and early twentieth-century art has many examples of the gundog breeds by artists who made a speciality of painting dogs.

The name terrier is derived from the Latin *terra*, meaning earth, and their work, as their name suggests, is to 'go to earth' and drive out rats, rabbits, foxes and other animals from their burrows or sets or to hold them there until they were dug out. Although terrier type dogs were, obviously, used elsewhere, most of the established modern breeds are of British origin, developed after fox-

LEFT

A Scottish Terrier and a Sealyham Terrier
by Lilian Cheviot (exhibited c. 1894-1902). Both these late nineteenth-century breeds are now best known as lively pets, but they were bred as tough, hard-working terriers. The Sealyham had its origins on an estate in Wales where, to survive to adulthood, a puppy had to prove itself small enough to go anywhere, undaunted by encountering other bad-tempered dogs. Its belligerence was tested when it reached one year old by presenting it with a polecat in a small pit with a narrow entrance. If it did not go straight in and attack, it would have been shot.

LEFT
The Day's Bag
by John Gifford (nineteenth century).
A Gordon Setter and English Setters
watch over the dead game.

ABOVE
By the Fireside
by Conradyn Cunaeus (1828-95).
The artist has included gun, powderhorn
and game bag, as a reminder of the day's
shooting. To make it clear that the day's
work is over a collar that has been taken
off has been left on the floor. The trio have
earned their fireside rest. From such
working ancestors as these come today's
pointers, setters and retrievers.

hunting became popular; few have long histories.

The Fox Terrier would run with the pack and come into its own if the fox went to earth. The Lakeland Terrier and Border Terrier had a similar role; the Welsh Terrier might also be used for otter hunting. Breeds were often very local: the Sealyham, for instance, was created on a Welsh estate where such dogs were used to tackle otters and polecats. Other breeds from around the British Isles include the Soft-coated Wheaten Terrier and Kerry Blue Terrier from Ireland, the Norwich Terrier from East Anglia and several Scottish breeds. The oldest Scottish terrier is probably the Skye, to which the Cairn, Dandie Dinmont, Scottish and West Highland

are all related. The Airedale, from Yorkshire, is the largest terrier – probably too large to go underground in true terrier fashion. It was bred to tackle otters and badgers and was one of the first breeds to be used as a police dog.

While terriers of no easily definable breed crop up in much earlier genre paintings of the countryside and a few which had become specialized at rat catching were painted to commemorate their skills, the modern breeds appear only in nineteenth- and twentieth-century pictures. They are breeds which were rapidly taken up as domestic dogs. The show and pet forms of today often look very different from the rougher working dogs of the past.

Toy Breeds and Family Pets

Most young animals have an appeal that evokes a protective instinct in adults, even of other species. We can imagine that as soon as dogs and people had learned to trust each other, puppies were petted and children played with them. This was probably an important stage in the process of domestication. The pattern of domestication and the development of different breeds discussed in the previous chapters has

been related to working dogs, but work is only one part of the human-dog relationship. The close bond between person and dog operates in both directions, and the dog becomes a colleague, companion and friend, as well as an animal carrying out a task.

The only contact for the dog that stays out on the mountainside to guard the flock year-round may be the shepherd, but dogs who can be taken home when work is done become part

of a larger pack – the family. Today, dog owners differ widely in how much of their lives they allow their dogs to share. Some see a dog's place as in a kennel outside the house, some allow the dog into only certain rooms indoors, while others encourage the dog to sleep on their own beds – or even in them. A dog may bring in dirt and shed hair over furnishings; large dogs, especially, may wreak havoc in a small space with their friendly

RIGHT

Giovanni Arnolfini and his Wife
by Jan Van Eyck (d. 1441).
*This double portrait, commissioned to
commemorate their wedding, is a
meticulous record of the moment, with the
onlookers reflected as witnesses in the
mirror on the back wall. However, its
naturalism incorporates many symbols
reflecting the couple's promises and hopes
for happiness, prosperity and children,
among which the dog in the foreground is
clearly intended as a symbol of fidelity.
However, this rough little terrier is surely
not an invented token animal but a dog
which was a real family pet.*

LEFT

The Return of Lodovico from Exile
*a fresco by Andrea Mantegna (1431-1506)
in the Camera degli Sposi of the Castello
di Corte in Mantua. Lodovico Gonzaga is
seen here with his family and household
and, as a natural part of the domestic
scene, what must be a favourite dog is
comfortably settled beneath his chair. The
artist has painted with meticulous detail
and the dog is shown with a short smooth
coat, but it appears to have a long ruff
around its neck. Is this a fringe attached
beneath his collar or a rather unusual
form of coat trim?*

exuberance and wagging tails. Our
modern ideas of hygiene and the
considerations of the house-proud
owner were of little importance in the
Middle Ages. The colourful
illuminations in medieval Books of
Hours often show dogs free to run
around the table at the banquets of
medieval nobles. In the hovels of the
poor, the close warmth of a dog's body
was probably very welcome on a cold
winter night.

A breed, such as the Foxhound,
bred to a life in kennels as part of a
hunting pack, does not adjust well to a
domestic environment. Most working
dogs, selectively bred for their
aptitude for particular tasks, can easily
become bored and ill-tempered if not
given the opportunity to exercise their
instinctive skills. Nevertheless, a
number of former working breeds are
now found only as show dogs and

domestic pets, adapting to the role of
companion. Often a smaller version of
the original breed has been developed
to make a more suitable domestic pet.
Some are recent creations, but others
go back many centuries; breeds of 'toy'
and companion dogs have been
around since ancient Egyptian times.

Ancient Egyptian 'toy' dogs – and
toy in a canine context simply means
small, no dog should be treated as a
plaything – cannot be identified as any
specific modern breed, although they

could be loosely described as a
small form of spitz. The same is true
of toy dogs depicted on Greek
ceramics and in Roman illustrations.
However, early in the first century
AD the Greek geographer and
historian Strabo described a beautiful
little dog, the *Canis Meliti,* as coming
from a town called Melita in Sicily. At
the same time, a Roman poet was
describing a little dog called Issa
belonging to Publius, Governor of
Malta (Latin Melita):

*Issa is more frolicsome than
Catulla's sparrow.
Issa is purer than a
dove's kiss.
Issa is gentler than a
young maid.
Issa is more precious than
oriental gems.
Fearing that darkness falling
on her days
Will snatch her away
for ever
Publius has had her painted.*

ABOVE
Miss Bowles
*by Sir Joshua Reynolds (1723-92). Although
Reynolds, first President of the Royal
Academy, often introduces dogs into his
pictures, they are usually only as an aid to the
composition, but here wide-eyed little Miss
Bowles and her toy spaniel share the picture.*

RIGHT
The Music Party
*attributed to Jan Miense Molenaer (1610-68).
A friendly little mongrel, obviously one of the
family, does not look entirely happy at being
made to dance to the fiddler's tune. Gripping a
dog's paws puts it under some duress, because
it is not free to control its own movement.*

What a pity we do not have that
picture, to confirm that Issa was the
same white, long-haired little dog that
has long been known as the Maltese. It
seems to be the oldest of the European
toy breeds. It became popular in
Britain at the time of the Tudors and
was described by Dr. John Caius, the
sixteenth-century royal physician who
wrote a classification of British dogs,
as: 'very small indeed and chiefly

sought after for the pleasure and
amusement of women who carried
them in their arms, their bosoms and
their beds'. Later Sir Joshua Reynolds
was to paint this breed as a cuddly
bundle of curly fur held on the lap of
Miss Nellie O'Brien in one of his
portraits of this fashionable
eighteenth-century London courtesan.

One mid-fourteenth century
manuscript depicts the poet Petrarch

with what appears to be a pug. This breed begins to appear frequently in the work of Dutch painters at the beginning of the seventeenth century. It became popular in the Dutch court and, when William of Orange became King of England, was taken across the North Sea to become fashionable there.

Dutch and Flemish artists painted many scenes of domestic life, among the peasantry and the bourgeoisie, in which all kinds of pet and working dogs can be seen, participating in the day-to-day activities of the home. Jan van Eyck's double portrait of Giovanni Arnolfini and his wife, painted in 1434, shows a little Griffon Terrier, a type which can also be seen in the works of Albrecht Dürer, Lucas Cranach and Hans Holbein. Little terriers like this most frequently occur in the work of Adriaen van Ostade, an early seventeenth-century painter. He seems to have had a particular liking for them and apparently owned a Griffon.

Griffons are missing from the work of southern European artists until much later. Indeed, miniature greyhounds (painted by van Eyck and others) also appear first in northern paintings. At a time when toy spaniels were painted only as the companions

ABOVE
Grace Before Meat
by Jan Havicksz Steen (1625-79).
This spaniel seems confident that a titbit will soon be coming his way if he is patient. Although one of the family, he is obviously his master's dog and looks well able to play his part on a day out after duck along the canals and polders of the Netherlands.

of the aristocracy in Italy, Spain or even England, they appear as the pets of the merchant classes in Dutch and Flemish pictures. Had the little toy breeds been established longer in the north or is this just a reflection of different fashions and the fact that northern artists more often had less aristocratic clients?

There is plenty of evidence of the pet dog among the great painters of the Italian Renaissance. Sandro Botticelli tucks a little white smooth-coated dog under the arm of one of the sons of Jethro in his frescoes of the life of Moses. Mantegna shows Ludovico Gonzago, Marquis of Mantua, sitting with his wife and surrounded by

family and household, with his dog lying in a basket beneath his chair. In the following century, Titian (Tiziano Veccellio) painted Ludovico's grandson, Federigo Gonzago, with a shaggy little dog sitting with one paw in the air on a table at his master's side. This is either a mongrel or a breed that is not now known, for

ABOVE
Jane, Lady Whichcote
*by Thomas Gainsborough (1727-88).
Gainsborough painted a number of
pictures which included white
Pomeranians, although the dog was then
very different from the diminutive breed
we know today. Among them was a
picture of a bitch and her puppy which
belonged to Karl Fredrich Abel, a
musician in the entourage of Queen
Charlotte. Gainsborough painted them in
return for lessons in playing the viola da
gamba from their owner. The large
Pomeranian was often used as a sheepdog,
which makes it appropriate in his painting
of the actress Mrs. Robinson in the role of
Perdita in* The Winter's Tale.

RIGHT
The Painter's Daughters
*by Thomas Gainsborough (1727-88).
The white dog this time is a Poodle and
probably the family pet. Poodles were a
retrieving breed, widely used to work in
water, bringing back shot ducks. The
breed is now known in three distinct sizes:
Standard (as here), Miniature and Toy –
which is under 28 cm (11 inches) high at
the shoulder.*

Titian includes dogs in many of his
pictures and most are clearly careful
portraits. He liked to paint children
with large dogs, the contrast
emphasizing the delicacy of the child,
but there are many little dogs, too,
such as a white dog with dropped ears
held by the youngest boy in a group
portrait of the Vedramin Family. He
often also includes dogs in his
mythical and allegorical subjects, such
as the huntress goddess's little dog
that hurls defiance at Actaeon and his
hound in his painting of Diana and

Actaeon. In a portrait of Alfonzo I d'Este he includes a tousle-haired little dog that some experts have suggested is a forerunner of the Papillon. A red-and-white toy spaniel appears in his portrait of the Duchess of Urbino and, most famously perhaps, a similar little dog curls near the feet of the goddess of love in his *Venus of Urbino*. Similar spaniels also appear in the works of his contemporary Jacomo Palma the Elder and in that of the younger painter Paolo Veronese.

Veronese must have liked painting dogs, for he includes them in many pictures. In 1537, because he gave dogs a prominent position in a painting of the Last Supper, he was called before the tribunal of the Inquisition and the painting was rejected. Veronese remedied the situation by changing the title of the painting and making it what we now know as *The Feast in the House of Levi*. This presumably made the dogs acceptable as part of a less sacred domestic scene.

Dogs which have been identified as an early form of the little Papillon, the Butterfly Spaniel which later became so popular in France, already appear in François Clouet's portrait of Marguerite de Valois, Queen of Francis I, and a portrait of one of her sons. They are seen again in paintings of balls during the reigns of Henry II and Henry III. They frequently appear in the work of Nicolas de Largillière, including a group portrait of Louis XIV and his family, and in the works of Jean-Antoine Watteau, Jean-Honoré Fragonard and other eighteenth-century French artists.

Papillons which were taken to the New World by the Spaniards are thought to be the origin of the tiniest of breeds, the Chihuahua. These were developed from dogs discovered in Mexico and the adjoining southern United States in the mid-nineteenth century, although other theories suggest that their ancestors may have been dogs introduced by the Chinese in the last century.

In the 1770s English artist Thomas Gainsborough painted a number of pictures depicting white spitz-type dogs, which have been variously

identified as Samoyeds, Keeshonds and Pomeranians. The artist called one picture *Pomeranian Bitch and Puppy* and, since these belonged to a German musician at the British court, it seems that they were examples of the north German breed. They are much bigger than the dogs which made the breed fashionable when Queen Victoria took an interest in them in the next century. Her kennels favoured dogs weighing 5.4-7.25 kg (12-16 lb), scarcely one third as heavy as Gainsborough's dogs. Today they are expected to be much, much smaller -- miniatures weighing only 1.8-2.5 kg (4-5 ½ lb).

Miniaturization has been applied to many types of dog to produce toy breeds: pinschers and poodles, as well as terriers and spaniels. Little dogs had great appeal as lapdogs, and breeders outdid each other to create dogs that were ever smaller. There was a warm welcome for small dogs from the Far East when they were introduced to Europe and America. The Chinese and Japanese miniature dogs had been recorded many centuries earlier. In 626 a pair that were only about 15 cm (6 inches) high were presented to the Chinese Emperor. It seems likely that they and

LEFT
Interior with a Lady at a Harpsichord
by Francesco Fieravino (Il Maltese) (1640-?).
In this rather contrived composition, more like a still-life assemblage than a natural setting, the dogs make their own comment on the duet being performed.

related small breeds originated in Japan.

The Pekingese, the Japanese Spaniel (or Japanese Chin) and the Pug are probably all developed from the same original stock. Some Japanese Chin may have reached Europe when the Portuguese started trading with Japan in the sixteenth century, the same time as the first Pugs seem to have appeared in Europe, but they are first recorded in the West when U.S. Commodore Perry brought some from Japan in 1853. One little dog called Tama ('Jewel' in Japanese) was brought back about two decades later by the French art collector Henri Cernuschi, who commissioned a portrait from Édouard Manet (who undertook several dog portraits). Tama was also painted twice by Auguste Renoir, making possible an interesting comparison between the approaches of the two artists.

The Pekingese were bred under the auspices of the Imperial Court and during the early nineteenth century, when they were a special interest of the Empress Dowager Cixi, their numbers reached many thousands. She wanted to have an animal which would suggest the ancient Buddhist

Head Study of a Yorkshire Terrier
by M. Cocker (nineteenth century).
The little Yorkie was bred as a ratting dog in the north of England by Yorkshire miners. It was originally much bigger and coarser than the dogs seen today. Breeders discovered that they could sell the smaller and daintier dogs to richer people as household pets and over the years, the toy dog of today emerged. Show dogs have a cascading curtain of silky fur from head to tail, but the coats of pet dogs can be trimmed to a more practical length and look more like their working ancestors.

Lion Dog, the legendary Foo Dog, and set the following criteria for the Pekingese: 'Let it wear the swelling cape of dignity around its neck. Let its forelegs be bent, so that it will not wish to wander far or leave our Imperial precincts. Let it be taught not to gad about. Let it be of the colour of the lion, to be carried in the sleeve of a yellow robe.'

Although it is possible that some Pekingese reached Europe earlier

(perhaps identifiable in Venice in the fifteenth century), the first recorded examples in the West were taken from Beijing by British officers following the burning and sacking of the Summer Palace during the Sino-Anglo-French conflict of 1860. One of these, appropriately named Looty, was presented to Queen Victoria and helped to establish a fashion for the breed in Britain.

The Shi Tzu, another dog with close links with the Pekingese, may be a Tibetan dog or may have originated in China. However, the Lhasa Apso, the little Tibetan Spaniel and the Tibetan Terrier are all of Tibetan origin. All these breeds found their way into western homes in the twentieth century.

In addition to these toy dogs, there are the many working breeds which

have now become more usual as domestic pets. Of course, there have always been many working dogs that have become a part of the household and fully share the life of the family.

Besides the obvious advantages of having a dog in the home as watchdog and guard, it has often been suggested that caring for a dog is a good way of teaching youngsters responsibility and an awareness of other creatures, but a dog can make a much wider contribution to our lives. Many a child will make the dog their confidant – the one friend with whom they can share all their hopes and fears with no risk of anyone else being told. It has been shown that handling a pet has a beneficial effect, reducing tension in the human, and contact with pets has been demonstrated to have therapeutic effects both on the physically sick and those under mental strain. Responsibility for a dog not only makes sure its owner gets some exercise in taking it out for walks, but there is evidence that people who have a dog, or any pet, recover more rapidly from illnesses and surgery. For anyone who lives alone they provide companionship and a friendly welcome and the additional interest and purpose they add to life can be a valuable contribution to our well-being.

RIGHT
Dogs and Peony
by Shen Chu'an, a late eighteenth-century Chinese painting on silk. A slightly older painting shows dogs more like our modern Pekingese but they are not mentioned in earlier Chinese texts. Were the dogs taken to the West poor specimens, not the true Imperial, type and is this what the Imperial dog originally looked like?

BELOW
A Saint Bernard and a Toy Dog
by Heinrich Sperling (1844-1924). The artist may have exaggerated a little, but there is a huge difference in size between the smallest and the largest dogs. The Miniature Pinscher should be 25.5-30.5 cm (10-12 inches) high at the shoulders and the Chihuahua is even smaller. The Saint Bernard has a minimum height of 69 cm (28 inches) and is often as much as 86 cm (34 inches). Great Danes, with a minimum height of 27.5 cm (30 inches), may be larger than the Saint Bernard, and with their erect carriage can look larger still.

RIGHT
A Musical Interlude
by Jan Verkolje (1630-93). Is this small spaniel the Dutch lady's pet, possessively keeping a wary eye on the behaviour of her fashionably dressed admirer, or has he arrived with the young man and is just eager that they should leave?

ABOVE
The Strolling Players
by Theophile-Emmanuel Duverger (1821-?).
Most dogs enjoy learning tricks and they have long
been a part of the entertainment provided by travelling
performers, buskers and circuses. Although today
many people would disapprove of dressing animals up,
it was often a feature of such shows.

ABOVE
A Staffordshire pottery figure of a King Charles Spaniel. Made by potteries in the heart of England in the mid nineteenth-century, such figures were popular chimney piece ornaments.

RIGHT
Boef can Keulen
*by Ditz (twentieth-century artist).
In the past, working Dachshunds used to
have rather longer, somewhat bandy legs,
but were still the familiar sausage shape.
They were ideally suited to following
quarry, such as badgers, underground;
their big feet were good for digging. Their
job was to go down and hold the animal at
bay, while their barking guided the
waiting hunters to the place to dig to get
the quarry out.*

LEFT
Spanish Woman in Grey
*by Natalia Gontcharova (1881-1952)
painted 1916. Despite its stylization, this
picture still captures the closeness between
the dog and its mistress, emphasized by
the echo of their triangular forms. The
Russian artist developed this 'Rayonist'
style with Mikhail Larionov, but she is
more widely known for her stage designs,
especially those for the Diaghilev Ballet.*

BELOW
Girl with a Dog
by L.S. Lowry (1887-1976).
This artist's simplified dog forms,
reminiscent of the canine images of
prehistoric cave painting, join the
'matchstick people' in many of his pictures
of life in the industrial towns of his native
Lancashire.

LEFT
Portrait of Bertrand
by Charles Verlat (1824-90).
This lively fellow is an Affenpinscher,
whose name means Monkey Terrier,
originally bred for ratting but now an
inquisitive and playful toy breed. They are
wary with strangers so, although small,
they make excellent watchdogs.

69

Faithful Friends

The loyalty of the dog to its master or mistress has been demonstrated so often that people tend to take it for granted, to accept that dogs long for approval and are instinctively programmed to defend the territory and protect the property and person of the one they have been conditioned to accept as leader. However, the devotion of the dog is amazing and we should never cease to wonder at it.

The dog's faithfulness was recognized long ago, inherent in the legends which sought to explain the partnership of dog and human, and was celebrated by poets and story-tellers. In the Odyssey, Homer's epic poem composed some 2,800 years ago, Odysseus, returning to his homeland after 20 years away, is recognized only by his dog. In historic times, in 480 BC when the Athenians were driven by the invading Persians to take refuge

on the island of Salamis, Xanthippos (father of Pericles) sailed with the fleet. His dog swam alongside the trireme, and was honoured in that the promontory where it was buried has since been known as Cynossema, meaning 'the Dog's Grave'.

From Welsh tradition comes the story of Gelert, hunting hound of the Prince Llewellyn ap Iorwerth. The prince, returning home one day, having left the dog on guard, is met by Gelert whose face is smeared with blood. Going in, followed by the dog, he finds his son's cradle overturned and the bedclothes blood-stained, too.

LEFT
Advice on the Prairie
by William Ranney (1813-57),
To the pioneers travelling out to the West and the homesteaders after the American Civil War, the dog was watchdog, guard, hunting assistant and friend.

BELOW
Queen Victoria's Favourite Pets
by Sir Edwin Landseer (1802-73).
This royal group includes Luath, the Deerhound, Eos, her husband Prince Albert's Greyhound, Dash, Victoria's King Charles Spaniel, and the Queen's parrot.

Calling the child he gets no answer and, thinking the boy has been savaged by the dog, kills it with his spear. The hound's dying cry wakes the baby and to his horror Llewellyn then discovers the body of a wolf, which Gelert has killed. The bloodstains that brought the death of faithful Gelert were gained in protecting the child. The story is a recurrent one, found in India at least a thousand years before, although not always associated with a dog. True or not, in Snowdonia the site of Gelert's grave is still marked in a valley near the village of Beddgelert.

The dog as protector from danger is classically presented in a painting exhibited in 1801 by Jeanne-Elisabeth Chaudet, a French artist who specialized in dramatic and rather sentimental pictures that frequently involve dogs and children. It shows a child asleep in a crib, with a dog sitting on guard beside it with its paws on a large and venomous snake that it has killed. Matthew Coates Wyatt's famous statue of Bashaw also shows a dog as the conqueror of a snake. In neither case is the artist known to be presenting any particular occasion, but such incidents must have been many.

There are many tales, too, of dogs who identify a thief or murderer. One, said to have occurred in France during the reign of Charles V in the fourteenth century, concerns Dragon, the dog of the knight Aubry de Mondidier. This knight was passing through the Forest of Bondy when he was attacked and murdered by a man whose armour rendered useless the dog's attempts at defence. The murderer buried the body and, for a time, the dog stayed by the grave. When no other person came, Dragon found his way to Paris and the home of a friend of Aubry. He managed to convince the man that he should follow him to the forest, where he led him to the grave and began to dig.

Later Dragon, usually gentle and friendly to everyone, suddenly sprang at a man's throat, and rumour began to spread that this man, Richard de Macaire, had been the unknown murderer. The king heard of it and ordered dog and accused man to be brought before him; again Dragon tried to avenge his master. Macaire could produce no convincing alibi for the time of the murder and it was decided that, following the custom of trial by combat, Macaire should face his accuser: Dragon. The contest took place on the Ile de Nôtre Dame and when Dragon once again had the murderer by the throat, de Macaire confessed and was then handed over to the executioner.

Cellini's assistants. They ignored his barking, even when he pulled off their bedclothes, only stirring when he grabbed them by the arm. Even then, they threw sticks at him, so he ran back to the shop and, finding the thief gone, chased after him. He managed to tear off the man's cape, but the thief called to others to help drive off the maddened dog and escaped.

Next morning, Cellini's staff saw the shop had been robbed. Fortunately the thief had not discovered jewels Cellini had for a piece he was making for Pope Clement, but he had taken all the clothes the journeymen had left there. Later, Cellini and his dog were passing through the Piazza Navona when a young man was being arrested, accused of another robbery. He was protesting his innocence and, since his accuser had little evidence, was on the point of being released, when the dog rushed across and went for him. The officers told Cellini to call him off or they would kill the dog, but as the retriever struggled, some packets fell from the man's hood. The other jeweller recognized them, and then a ring which Cellini recognized also fell out. Cellini allowed the dog to renew his attack until the man confessed and restored what he had stolen.

In the entrance hall of the London salesrooms of Phillips, the auctioneers, a painting of a small boy and a dog has pride of place. This is Master Harry Phillips with his dog Friend. The grown-up Harry founded the company in 1796, and Friend is reputed to have saved his life. A painting by George Moreland and a popular print made from it also commemorate the event. It is difficult to be sure what breed is intended here – could it be a collie or is it meant to be a Newfoundland, a breed which was used to help haul nets and is usually a powerful swimmer. A few years later Landseer made many paintings of Newfoundlands and the black and white type he depicted now carries his name – the Landseer. His *Off to the Rescue* and *A Distinguished Member of the Humane Society* are a direct tribute to the dog's life-saving

For an example of the thief identified we have the account of Italian artist Benvenuto Cellini, concerning his own dog – he calls it 'a fine retriever' but we do not know its name – which surprised a thief who had broken into the goldsmith's shop. Unable to grapple with the man, who was armed, the dog rushed around the rest of the house trying to wake

The Painter and his Dog
by William Hogarth (1697-1764)
The dog which so prominently shares
Hogarth's self-portrait is Trump. The
second of two pug dogs he owned – The
first was named simply 'Pug'. So there is
no doubt of the type though its appearance
has changed considerably to become that
of the modern show dog.

RIGHT
A Man and his Dogs
by Richard Ansdell (1815-85).
Three sporting dogs, including a
Deerhound and a little Terrier, with
a Scottish gillie, are all still watchful
although their master has fallen
asleep on the hillside at the end of an
exhausting day.

reputation. The Humane Society was an organization founded in 1774 to encourage the use of first-aid and resuscitation techniques to help victims of shipwreck and drowning. It was not until 1824, the year in which Landseer exhibited his portrait of Neptune, another heroic-looking Newfoundland, that the first animal humane society, the (soon to become Royal) Society for the Prevention of Cruelty to Animals, was founded.

Perhaps the most important way in which the modern dog gives exemplary service to its owner is in guiding the blind. The use of dogs by the blind has a long history, perhaps being originally as much for protection of their owners and of any alms they may have been given as for helping to lead them. The planned training of dogs specifically as guides is comparatively recent. Although Johann Lein, founder of the Institute for the Blind in Vienna, set out principles for training such dogs back in 1819, this was not taken up. The modern Seeing-Eye movement began in 1916, when a German doctor walking with a wounded soldier was suddenly called to an emergency and

left his German Shepherd Dog with the patient. It began to rain before he returned and he found that the dog had led the blind man to shelter. From that began special training of dogs to aid the blinded of World War I. German war-blinded soldiers were presented with fully-trained guide-dogs and there were also experiments with dogs in France. In Switzerland an American woman, Mrs. Harrison Eustis, started a school and the movement known as *L'Oeil qui Voit* ('The Seeing Eye'). A dog called 'Buddy' was matched to Morris Frank and in 1928 became their first American guide dog, although John Sinykin, a German Shepherd breeder who had trained a dog for a blind U.S. Senator, had also set up a school, the Master Eye Institute, in 1926.

The British Guide Dogs for the Blind Association was founded in 1930 and other national organizations followed. German Shepherds, Golden Retrievers and Labradors have proved the most suitable breeds, with bitches (who are less easily distracted by smells and other dogs) usually chosen, although all dogs are neutered before training.

The final devotion of the dog, watching over a deceased owner or as mourner has been the subject of many paintings and is exemplified in two dogs, one in Scotland and one in Japan whose stories are commemorated by permanent memorials.

In Edinburgh, it was a little Skye Terrier, called Bobby, who followed the mortal remains of his master to the churchyard at Greyfriars in 1858. The dog refused to leave the spot until he died ten years later. Today a little statue stands on a plinth on the roadside nearby.

On the other side of the world in Japan, an Akita called Hachikou went to Tokyo's Shibuya subway station every day to greet his master as he came home from his work as a professor at the University of Tokyo. On the day the professor died, the dog waited for him until midnight and then returned home alone. He continued to go and wait at the station each day for the next nine years until his own death in 1934. A collection raised funds for a statue at the station exit which commemorates his devotion.

ABOVE

Play Fellows

by Charles M. Schreiber (exhibited 1868-1901). The Pug was probably originally a Chinese breed, although popular in Europe from the seventeenth century. The modern type has a flatter and more wrinkled face than this alert young dog. This has created a breed that can be very snuffly, especially on hot days, when its shortened nasal passages may make its breathing laboured.

RIGHT

Harry Phillips and Friend.

Neither painter nor date for the work are known, but this picture commemorates a young boy and the dog that saved him from drowning towards the end of the eighteenth century. In 1796 the boy, grown up, was the founder of a London auction house, where this picture is given a place of honour.

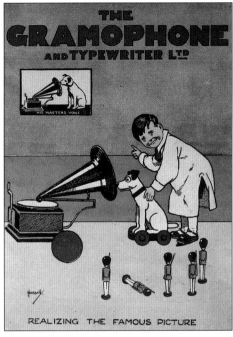

REALIZING THE FAMOUS PICTURE

ABOVE

An advertisement

*drawn by John Hassall (1868-1948),
for the Gramophone and Typewriter
Company Ltd., makers of 'His Master's
Voice' records. Hassall began as a farmer
in Manitoba before becoming a painter.
The 'famous picture' was a painting by
the otherwise little-known British artist
Francis Barraud (1856-1924), which
showed the behaviour of his pet dog,
Nipper, when a recorded voice was played
back on an Edison phonograph. The
picture was turned down by the Royal
Academy for the Summer Exhibition in
1899, but Barraud registered it as a
copyright and offered it to the Edison Bell
Company. They refused it, but the
Gramophone and Typewriter Company
agreed to buy it, provided that the Edison
machine with its cylinder was painted out
and replaced by their own new flat disk
machine. From the beginning of 1900, the
amended image began to appear on the
company's advertising and record labels
in the form seen here on the wall.*

BELOW
The Old Shepherd's Chief Mourner
by Sir Edwin Landseer (1802-73).
The poignant image, so typical of the
romantic feeling of this period but entirely
lacking the cloying sentimentality it often
produced, is a fine example of the artist's
work and among the best known of all dog
paintings.

The best friend a man has in this world may turn against him and become his enemy. His son or daughter that he has reared with loving care may prove ungrateful. Those who are nearest and dearest to us, those whom we trust with out happiness and our good name, may become traitors to their faith. the money that a man has, he may lose. It flies away from him, perhaps when he needs it most. A man's reputation may be sacrificed in a moment of ill-considered action. The people who are prone to fall on their knees to do us honor when success is with us may be the first to throw the stone of malice when failure settles its cloud upon our heads. The one absolutely unselfish friend that a man can have in this selfish world, the one that never deserts him and the one that never proves ungrateful or treacherous is his dog.

Gentlemen of the Jury, a man's dog stands by him in prosperity and in poverty, in health and in sickness. He will sleep on the cold ground, where the wintry winds blow and the snow drives fiercely, if only he may be near his master's side. He will kiss the hand that has no food to offer, he will lick the wounds and sores that come in encounters with the roughness of the world. He guards the sleep of his pauper master as if he were a prince. When all other friends desert he remains. When riches take wings and reputation falls to pieces, he is as constant in his love as the sun in its journey through the heavens. If fortune drives the master forth an outcast in the world, friendless and homeless, the faithful dog asks no higher privilege than that of accompanying him to guard against danger, to fight against his enemies, and when the last scene of all comes, and death takes the master in its embrace and his body is laid away in the cold ground, no matter if all other friends pursue their way, there by his graveside will the noble dog be found, his head between his paws, his eyes sad but open in alert watchfulness, faithful and true even to death.

Senator George Vest, inscribed on the memorial to Old Drum in Warrensbury, Missouri.

Acknowledgements
The author would like to thank Wendy Boorer for her advice.

All pictures courtesy of The Bridgeman Art Library, London; except the following which were supplied by
Viewpoint Projects: 15, 16, top and bottom, 30 left, 69 bottom.

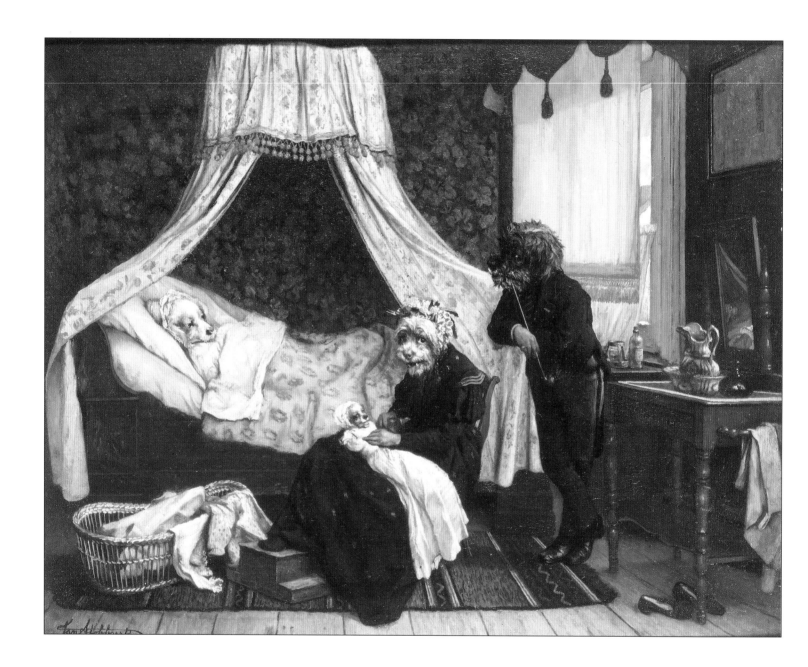

ABOVE
The Newly Born
by Jan Stobbaerts (1838-1914).
This painting is an odd piece of
anthropomorphism. What do these dog-
headed humans represent? Is it a comment
on human domesticity and proud
parenthood? It certainly suggests that the
artist felt a great affection towards dogs.